D1412290

handmade
christmas

COUNTRY LIVING

handmade
christmas

Text by Mary Seehafer Sears
Photography by Keith Scott Morton
Styling by Amy Leonard

HEARST BOOKS

A Division of Sterling Publishing Co., Inc.

NEW YORK

Every effort has been made to ensure that all the information in this book is accurate. However, due to differing conditions, tools, and individual skills, the publisher cannot be responsible for any injuries, losses, and/or other damages that may result from the use of the information in this book.

This book was previously published as a hardcover under the title *Country Living Handmade Christmas: Decorating Your Tree and Home*.

PRODUCED BY SMALLWOOD & STEWART, INC., NEW YORK CITY
Editor: Carrie Chase
Crafts Editor: Deri Reed
Art Director: Debbie Sfetsios
Designer: Alexandra Maldonado

Library of Congress Cataloging-in-Publication Data
Available upon request.

10 9 8 7 6 5 4 3 2 1

First paperback edition 2003
Published by Hearst Books
A Division of Sterling Publishing Co., Inc.
387 Park Avenue South, New York, NY 10016

Country Living and Hearst Books are trademarks owned by Hearst Magazines Property, Inc., in USA, and Hearst Communications, Inc., in Canada.

www.countryliving.com

Distributed in Canada by Sterling Publishing
c/o Canadian Manda Group, One Atlantic Avenue, Suite 105
Toronto, Ontario, Canada M6K 3E7
Distributed in Australia by Capricorn Link (Australia) Pty. Ltd.
P.O. Box 704, Windsor, NSW 2756 Australia

Text set in Galliard

Printed in Singapore

ISBN 1-58816-292-3

table of contents

foreword

Christmas and the traditions associated with this holiday have their own special magic—the heart-warming sounds of carolers singing old but familiar songs of the season, the excitement of decorating the tree with brightly colored ornaments collected over the years, and, of course, the anticipation of Santa's arrival and the unexpected surprises that he is certain to bring.

We created this book with these deeply held feelings and memories in mind. You'll discover ideas and projects for every aspect of the holiday—from decorating the tree with handmade ornaments, to making gift wrap and tags that give even the simplest gift the presence of your personality, to adorning the house with decorations that will become part of your holiday tradition over the years to come.

In the end, of course, the reason we do all this planning, creating, and decorating is to shower our homes, our family, and our friends with love. And what is more meaningful and loving than something crafted by hand? Christmas reminds us of the joys of sharing, and we hope you find these projects inspiring as you open your heart and home to the holiday spirit and to those you love.

— Nancy Mernit Soriano, Editor-in-Chief

introduction

If you believe life is a celebration, then each year's crescendo is Christmas. The air fairly buzzes with anticipation and excitement. At the old Russian Tea Room in New York, the Christmas decorations stayed up year-round. That's the spirit! Christmas is more than a single day on the calendar. For some, it's a bona fide year-round holiday.

The Christmas spirit washes over us just as the tide of Thanksgiving recedes, and if we're lucky it never fully disappears. The spirit tiptoes along on summer vacation, inspiring organized sorts to take the Christmas picture and buy special gifts not found at home. A glimpse of vintage ornaments at a fall antiques fair starts ideas percolating for decorating the tree in December. We buy Christmas cards at first appearance, long before we've figured out where last year's list might be. And so it goes.

This book about creating a handmade holiday should make your Christmas particularly splendid. We've divided the book into three chapters—the house, the tree, and gift wraps. Every page is filled with suggestions and projects for crafting your own homemade Christmas. Some of the ideas are practical and some are lighthearted. All are easy to do, and some are wonderful for kids to join in on. Many projects call for scraps found around the house. Making things by hand—even one thing—will provide a fuller Christmas for you and your family, whether that family is a houseful of raucous relatives, a few close friends, or just you and the kitty cat.

chapter one

a homespun holiday

When it comes to **decorating** the house for Christmas, my family and I like to do it all at once. We pull the ornament boxes out of the basement or attic, haul them to the living room, and take everything out willy-nilly. Candles with hollyberry ruffs hit the tables, the **Santa** coasters are dealt out like cards, and by the end of the afternoon there's holiday potpourri in the bathroom and a wreath on the front door. The cats lob **jingle bells** around the living room and even though the bells eventually vanish under the sofa, there's no denying it's Christmas!

There are other ways to approach the holidays. Some people like to take it a bit slow, starting with a Saturday afternoon devoted to **card-making** and list-updating, then gradually taking on more projects. Cookie dough is made and frozen the following week; gift wrapping and decorating supplies inventoried. The holiday **spirit** cases its way through the house, eventually touching every room. In the end, no matter how you approach it, the result is the same: a home that is welcoming and festive for friends and family.

The trick to a wonderful Christmas just might begin with making a list of the things you want your Christmas to include, and then finding ways of making the most important dreams come true. This is something you can do on your own, although it might be more fun to daydream aloud with other people, perhaps in a workshop at church, with everyone coming away with a pretty picture in mind. Close your eyes and envision the best holiday scenario ever. Maybe you'll realize you've always wanted to roast an enormous goose for Christmas dinner. Or perhaps your fantasy is to cut down your own tree and make plum pudding, fruitcakes, and a dozen different Christmas cookies. You can make your dream real even if you don't have lots of time: Just take advantage of the multitude of time-savers available. Buy premade Christmas swags. Hire a teenager to address your Christmas cards. Throw a cookie baking party or—heavens!—buy cookie dough in a tube and put your energies into the cookie decorating, which is really the fun part anyway. In the end, of course, what you want is a memorable, peaceful Christmas. How you did it can be your secret.

And, always, remember the guiding principle of Christmas: More is better. And this doesn't mean presents. More love. More kindness. More hope.

Deck the halls

'Tis the season to garnish the house! Grand decorating schemes often stir up more stress than satisfaction. Instead, concentrate on little touches throughout the house that will cheer you with their simplicity.

A bucket of greenery topped with dried flowers, cookie cutters lined up on windowsills, fat sugar cookies in a silver dish—accents like these quickly bring a cheerful note to every corner. Set out a bowl of oranges to add color to a hallway or dining room, perhaps studding them with cloves for extra fragrance. Use gold, silver, or plaid ribbon throughout the house, woven through banisters, for example, or draped around mirrors. Capitalize on the architectural features in your home: Window frames or picture frames can be swagged with strings of bead balls or garlands. Tuck sprigs of pine behind picture or mirror frames.

Handmade treasures, including needlework ornaments crafted from tea-stained fabric, grace the branches of this evergreen tree, whose trunk is hidden by a stately basket. Birds' nests on the mantel and a Christmas throw on the table enhance the warm, rustic air of the room.

A collection of little chairs can become a stage for improvised decorations: a bowl of citrus fruits with a collar of pine, a basket of oranges, pinecones, and cranberry ropes (the berries can be either wooden or real), or a family of dolls and bears bundled up in blankets. Keep the lighting low and atmospheric by placing electric candles with four-watt decorative night lights in the windows or using real candles everywhere.

To "pump up" the look of any room, think in multiples and use anything that shines and sparkles. Small lighted trees make wonderful decorations; an odd number, like three, five, or seven, creates a tiny tabletop forest. Hang twin wreaths on the wall side by side, or a small wreath inside a larger one. Give an illusion of fluffiness by hanging a single wreath in front of a tall mirror, perhaps above the dining-room buffet. Prop a large mirror against the wall to reflect a scene, and then lean another one against it.

In the kitchen, you'll want to pull out the Santa cookie jar, of course, and the cheese spreaders decorated with reindeer, the red and green bowls, and the Christmas-tree platter. And if you also light a candle each morning, it will set a relaxed tone during the seasonal rush. It will keep you feeling calm and peaceful, no matter how hectic the atmosphere.

In the dining room, red, gold, or beeswax candles in the chandelier or red velvet bows tied around a collection of candlesticks are a cheering touch. Hang small white origami doves from a crystal chandelier, or handpainted

color schemes

If your Christmas decor needs uplifting, vary your color scheme. Try choosing a single color for the tree: all silver or all gold, for example. Or emphasize a color theme for the whole house: Start with the ornaments on the tree and the linens on the dining table, and perhaps extend your chosen colors to throw pillows or blankets on the couch. If you narrow the range of colors the overall look can be very striking. Consider these holiday palettes:

- red, green, and white—the traditional tones of the season

- pale pink, silver, and ivory—a restrained, sophisticated choice

- lemon yellow and evergreen—bright and sunny, especially in warmer climates

- lavender, purple, and sage green—glorified country

- silver and gold, brass and pewter, copper and bronze—sparkling and royal

- crimson and gold—stately and elegant

- silver, blue, and green—cool and relaxing, great for snow country

ornaments from a wrought-iron one. Festoon a gold chandelier with bunches of red pepperberries. Tie green bows around lamp bases and dust the lampshades with glitter (which can be vacuumed up later, with the pine needles).

A wintry bedroom is a perfect retreat from all the Christmas festivities, but can still reflect a holiday air. For a warm sleep, make up the beds with cozy flannel or knit sheets

in seasonal colors. Trim the open ends of pillowcases with jumbo green and red rick-rack, set about five inches in from the edge. Put tabletop trees in the bedrooms to give everyone in the house a chance at personalized tree-trimming. Or use large rosemary plants—with their spiky leaves that resemble a fir's—which can become miniature, mock Christmas trees when accented with tiny little gold bows and pepperberries.

If you have any knack for sewing, pillows are a great way to express your Christmas spirit. A pillow is a blank chalkboard, ready to be decorated to dress up a chair or sofa. Tiny hand-size scented balsam or spice pillows can be tucked into upholstered chairs, on shelves, in bookcases, or piled in a silver bowl on a front hall table for guests to take home.

When making pillows, start with a sumptuous fabric: Velvet, long associated with festivity, is soft and touchable. Satin, taffeta, and woven brocades are other opulent choices. Bright felts are fun and require no hemming. To give any pillow a gossamer shimmer, slip it into a sheer silk organza bag you've stitched yourself, as slick as a glaze of ice.

If you've put off redecorating for one reason or another, the holidays give you the impetus to bring these projects to the fore. The onslaught of holiday company is a great motivator, so hire the painter or pull out the

capture the moment

Taking a moment to record times spent together gives us something to look back on, and Christmas is the logical time to seize such an opportunity. Establishing such rituals at Christmas ensures that at least once a year, a permanent remembrance will be created.

▲ Take a family photograph in front of the tree every Christmas Eve and capture the people and the tree at their holiday best.

▲ Don't let a visitor leave without signing a holiday guest book.

▲ Make sketches of each other and store them in a Christmas scrapbook.

▲ Write prediction letters to be read New Year's Eve next year.

▲ Write the names of family members on rocks and lay them in the garden.

ladders and go on a painting spree. If you don't want to do the whole house, paint the dining-room trim a warm winter red to give the downstairs a quick update.

Every Christmas brings yet another holiday trend, like the outdoor icicle lights that appeared a few years ago. Buy at least one new Christmas item every year, perhaps a souvenir picked up on vacation, to keep your home looking fresh. Your holiday tradition probably includes unpacking beloved decorations—mingling in new ones will rejuvenate this process. Holiday decorations should flow and change, or a house becomes stagnant.

Trimming the outdoors

Your house extends a welcome even before you do, so make the outside as pretty as the inside. For a warm first impression, start with the front door. If it needs repainting, this is the time to try a bright cardinal red or deep evergreen color. Polish the brass, and make sure the doorbell works!

There's no better way to spell out the fact that the season is upon us than hanging a

Let no spot go untouched by holiday fun: At the side of a house, miniature mittens, baby's breath, and pinecones decorate cypress and spruce trees riding in a 1930s primitive canoe. The tiny handcrafted log cabin makes this a houseboat of sorts. A dried herb and berry wreath accents the weathered wood.

wreath on the front door. It can seem to light up an entire street. An artificial wreath—decorated with sophisticated gold ribbons, frosted fruits, and jewel-colored ball ornaments—can work its holiday magic just as well as a fresh one. A wreath almost as wide as the door perfectly expresses the opulence of the season and sets a party mood. Other ways to extend a welcome at the front door: Hang some sleigh-bells so they jingle with each guest's arrival. Tuck a coronet of oak or maple leaves around the knocker. Buy a new doormat. Shine a light on the entrance.

Out in front, light a snow-banked walkway with ice "lanterns." Make them by freezing water in nested bowls: Fill the bigger container with water to two inches from the top; slip in the smaller bowl and weight it down with sand or pie weights. Crisscross the bowls with tape to hold them in place. Freeze solid, unmold the "ice bowl," and place a lit votive in the indent. Or outline the path with luminarias—votive candles in sand-weighted brown or white paper bags.

On a still night, fill several spanking-new galvanized watering cans with freshly fallen snow and tamp down. Press two or three tall dripless cranberry tapers into the snow-filled cans and light them. Set the cans on top of a snowbank or along the sidewalk. They will shine like fistfuls of light.

The fireplace

All eyes are on the fireplace at Christmas time, the scene of Santa's descent! A brass bucket on the hearth full of fatwood kindling tied with tartan ribbons looks inviting and keeps the fire roaring.

Decorate the mantel with clusters of your favorite things: groupings of Santas, bells, pinecones, stockings will have a strong impact en masse. Arrange candlesticks of brass, glass, or silver next to slim, colored bottles that can also serve as candle holders. Instead of the usual tapers of red, green, or burgundy, try classic white, bayberry, or the palest golden-yellow candles.

No fireplace should be empty at Christmas time. If yours is not a working one, perch a group of lit votives in glass cups on birch logs piled in the fireplace. Or fill it with a fan of evergreen boughs, or a large basket overflowing with oversize pinecones.

White candles, long-stemmed tulips, and poinsettias light up a living room. A Scotch pine, shorn of its lower branches, becomes a tall-stemmed topiary wearing golden ribbon around its trunk. Dried hydrangeas stud the tree and a boxwood wreath criss-crossed with grapevines. Think of natural decorations like these as winter, not just holiday, decorations—they can be left in place for a month or more, with only the fresh flowers needing replacement.

Embellishing a store-bought fir wreath—with cookie cutters, ornaments, dried flowers, or things tied to a theme (seed packets and miniature garden tools, for example)—is one of the easiest ways to add personality to a wreath. Try these ideas for making wreaths from different forms:

▲ Glue pinecones to a wire base with a hot glue gun, leaving room at the top for a hanging bow, then spray paint the pinecones antique gold. Insert "stars" of dried Queen Anne's lace between the pinecones.

▲ For an untamed wreath, wrap grapevine branches (known as grape canes) into a large circle, about two feet in diameter, weaving the ends in to conceal them.

▲ With a paddle of thin green floral wire, attach greenery, such as holly, boxwood, fir, or balsam—perhaps mixing them with heather, juniper berries, pinecones, or hay— to straw or wire forms. Tie on a raffia bow, or hang the wreath from a window with red gingham ribbon, its ends draping down.

▲ On a Styrofoam circle form, attach boxwood crisscrossed with grapevines and studded with dried hydrangeas.

▲ Pin to a straw wreath—or tie on with yarn—small, brightly colored mittens.

▲ From a wire ring wreath, hang antique ornaments and miniature books with fishing line; drape strands of gold beads and juniper berries over the wreath form.

Candles

Never underestimate the power of candles. They set a room aglow like nothing else, and if you trim the wicks before you light them, they'll burn more cleanly. Dim all the lights in the house and create instant atmosphere from the flickering light of a collection of candles in different sizes. Candelabras, wall sconces, glass votives—bring out as many candle holders as you can. If you have a variety of holders, unite them by using just a single color of candle. Placing some of them in front of mirrors or near other reflective surfaces (such as silver bowls or glass balls) multiplies their effect. Just be sure to keep the flames clear of the tree or any flammable decorations.

Votive candles grouped together are an inexpensive way to transform a room, or, for a lovely coffee-table centerpiece, float holly leaves and votive candles molded in different shapes in a glass bowl of water.

Candles look best in matching colors. On a mantel, gather multiple sizes—some short, some tall—and arrange them on one side. Or line up the candles from left to right in strict precision, like choristers. Employ little terra-cotta pots to hold stout candles and nestle them among strands of ivy to create a natural scene.

The holiday table

There's a reason they call it the groaning board, especially at Christmas. The table—in the kitchen, dining room, or great room—is the site of many delicious meals and much merriment. One creative party-giver sets her table with a bright red Christmas tablecloth every year, and guests sign their name and the date on the cloth when they sit down to dine. Later, she highlights the names with white embroidery floss, and now has a signature cloth with many memories attached.

Tie the look of your Christmas table to memories—set a dark wooden table with your grandmother's lace tablecloth and the cranberry-glass goblets that appeared on her table for decades, and bring out your mother's collection of pink transferware plates for Christmas dinner. Or create a centerpiece for the table from a basket wrapped with a burgundy velvet ribbon and filled with lemons and limes or tiny Christmas trees, or use a glass plate piled high with sugared fruit (see page 41).

Christmas with animals

Animals are a big part of the Christmas celebration, from the farm animals in manger scenes to sweater-clad teddy bears under the tree. If you love animals, let your house reflect that love. Give your pet's bed a fresh look by stitching a new washable cover made from holiday-motif cotton. Make a neck scrunchie for your dog or cat (be sure it is very loose so it's easy to pull out of if it gets caught on something).

Place out of reach poisonous plants that animals (and children) might nibble at. These include Christmas rose, holly, mistletoe berries, philodendron, diffenbachia, spider plant, oleander, croton, poinsettia, and Jerusalem cherry. Chocolate is poisonous to dogs, so don't leave any boxed goodies and candy dishes unattended.

Taking time to care for wildlife expresses the giving spirit of Christmas. Plug in a

natural decorations

Old-fashioned Christmas celebrations and natural decorations go hand in hand. Don't overlook the power of a basket of pine boughs and baby pumpkins, or cranberry and popcorn ropes strung on string or dental floss. Other natural decorations: curly twigs, butcher's-broom (*Ruscus*), cones, berries in a bed of straw, artichokes, Queen Anne's lace, pyracantha berries, bittersweet, wheat, Scandinavian straw horses (*julbucks*) and straw stars, gourds, branches and leaves, pods, fruits, nuts, a bowl full of acorns, oranges or clementines, leaves and evergreen boughs. And finally, a piece of coal sticking out of a stocking is sure to amuse.

warmer to keep the birds' drinking water from freezing. Feed the birds suet, raisins, cranberries, sunflower seeds, peanuts, and cracked corn, and decorate the feeder with a big red bow. String peanuts in the shell on dental floss to make an edible garland for the squirrels.

The plants of Christmas

Paper-white narcissus are as much an emblem of Christmas as new-fallen snow—but far easier to orchestrate! Begin to force paper-whites about three to five weeks before you want them to bloom. Fill a container that does not have drainage holes with pebbles, gravel, or coarse sand to reach just an inch below the top. Anchor a half-dozen or so bulbs (depending on the container's size) in the pebbles, and add enough water to barely touch the bottoms of the bulbs. Maintain this water level and place the container in a cool (55–60°F), dark place until shoots develop—about two weeks. (A tie-top black plastic garbage bag, with the bowl of bulbs inside, acts as a mini greenhouse, holding in moisture and providing the necessary darkness.) When roots form and shoots emerge, bring them into indirect light, where they will bloom and spread their heady scent throughout the house for about two weeks. Force more bulbs every few weeks throughout the winter for a continuous series of flowers.

The Christmas cactus is another holiday plant that can be coaxed into bloom for the holidays, its long arching arms tipped with red or white flowers. Like narcissus, it needs enough darkness and cold to break dormancy and bloom, so stop watering a week before Halloween, and put the plant in a cool place that's totally dark at night. Water only enough to keep the plant alive, and after six weeks acclimate it over a week or so to warmer temperatures to encourage blooms.

The perennial Christmas favorite, the poinsettia, is a fairly fragile plant. To insure that it blooms throughout the season, give it plenty of sunlight, and water moderately. When buying a poinsettia, look for mature plants with dense, dark green foliage all the way down the stem. The plants should have little or no green around the edges of the bracts—the colorful (red, white, pink, peach, yellow, or mottled) leaves that surround the poinsettia's tiny flowers.

Swags, wreaths, and garlands

Evergreens, holly, ivy, and mistletoe bring your house to life at Christmastime. Long before the Christian era, man honored the changing

A luxuriant garland of laurel and pine, wrapped with cord painted silver and gold, loops gracefully along the balustrade. A burst of dried hydrangeas and a wide tapestry ribbon accent the newel post. The decorations seem as natural as the wall mural depicting a scenic view of early 19th-century Casco Bay in Maine.

seasons in ancient pagan festivals, and the greens that were a part of these festivals have now been incorporated into the Christmas tradition. Mistletoe, once thought to have destructive power, is now a symbol of love and peace. Holly is said to scare away evil spirits and protect against lightning. Ivy is a symbol of faithfulness. If you're superstitious, have more holly than ivy in your Christmas decorations to ward off bad luck in the coming year.

Wiring strands of fresh-cut boughs together to make a swag is well and good (and smells great), but few of us set aside time for such peaceful pleasures. During this busy season, speed the process by purchasing premade lengths of pine, balsam fir, or laurel and draping them along every conceivable surface for a touch of country elegance. For a special effect, intertwine two ropes of different greenery. The more ambitious can festoon the greenery with eucalyptus wands, ribbons, fruit, silver or gold leaves, dried flowers, herbs, cones, cinnamon sticks, or berries. Use floral picks—which resemble weighty toothpicks, pointed at both ends—to attach decorative baubles and berries to your swag. Pierce the decoration with one end of the floral pick, and stab the other end into the swag. Wrap the swag around the banister, or hang it along the side of the staircase in graceful swoops.

To give the holiday touch to doors and windows indoors and out, wire boxwood cuttings to a slender rope and tack the rope around the frames.

Reality check

Preparing the house for the holidays should be an affair of the heart, not a rat race. Rather than tying yourself to a weekly timetable of things to do, consider these more relaxed options:

When you're sitting down alone . . .

▲ address your Christmas cards;

▲ string popcorn and cranberries;

▲ plan the holiday dinner menus;

When you're sitting with your family . . .

▲ create a list of things you could make each other, and avoid catalogs and stores entirely;

▲ write down three things you want to do over the Christmas holidays as a family: skating, seeing a particular movie, visiting friends or relatives everyone likes;

▲ delegate . . . Your husband and kids might like to put the outside lights up, stand in line at the post office for stamps, or plan and prepare Christmas dinner.

Fragrant paper-white narcissus spring from a wooden window box topped with a frizz of moss. The bulbs were forced in bowls of stones and water, then transferred to the crate once they began to sprout. Golden wired ribbon festoons the breakfront, and helps keep fragile narcissus stems upright.

window snowflakes

New-fallen snowflakes made from wavy pipe cleaners or cut paper are as fresh as the real thing—and last far longer, no matter what the temperature. The lacy paper cutouts are snipped from plain white folded paper. You might also want to try shiny shelf paper, metallic paper, tissue paper, or solid-colored gift wrap. The pipe cleaner snowflakes are made by cutting and gluing white wavy pipe cleaners into starry shapes. Stenciling snowflakes on the glass is a third possibility: Make stencils from heavy cardstock or manila folders and use white shoe polish, poster paint, or Glass Wax as your medium.

▲ For each paper snowflake, cut an 8-inch square of paper (or larger). Fold the paper in half, then in quarters, then in eighths. With scissors, cut shapes into the sides to form a snowflake. The more you cut, the more delicate a pattern you create (you'll need to leave some folded edges uncut, however). Unfold the paper and tie a string to the top. Attach the hole reinforcers to the end of the string and hang the snowflake from the window muntin. Trim excess thread.

▲ For the simplest pipe cleaner snowflake, cross three pipe cleaners at their centers and glue. Make more elaborate snowflakes by cutting pipe cleaners and gluing the pieces to the centers of four- or six-point flakes, always making symmetrical designs. On each snowflake, make a small loop at the end of one pipe cleaner of each snowflake and tie on a piece of string. Attach hole reinforcers to the ends of the strings and hang the snowflakes from the window muntin. Trim excess thread.

❖   ❖   ❖

MATERIALS

white lightweight paper

string

white hole reinforcers (available in office supply stores)

white chenille wavy pipe cleaners (available in craft stores)

TOOLS

quick-drying craft glue

scalloped christmas
tablecloth

This tablecloth provides the perfect setting for a holiday tea party. We've chosen a ticking-stripe cloth, but a festive print would work, too. Or use the same scallop edging technique to make a tree skirt.

MATERIALS

mattress-ticking fabric and matching thread

cotton fabric for lining

3/8-inch-wide ribbon

buttons

TOOLS

newsprint for pattern

compass

1. The challenge in making a scalloped border is getting equal-sized scallops to fit along each edge. Measure your table, adding 7 to 8 inches for drop on all sides, and make a pattern from the newsprint. Calculate the number of scallops you will need for each side—keeping in mind that scallops measuring 2 to 5 inches are usually scaled right for most tables. If your table is round, divide the pattern into quadrants and with the compass draw an equal number of circles along the edge of each quadrant. If your table is square, divide the width of the pattern by 12. Use this number and draw a square on the pattern this many inches in from the edges. Draw a row of six side-by-side circles centered along the inside line, each circle with a radius that equals the width of the pattern divided by 12. If your table is rectangular, you will need to space the scallops along the long edges and then perhaps trim the pattern to fit a smaller number of same-size scallops along the short edges.

2. Using the paper pattern, cut out one piece of ticking fabric and one piece of lining fabric. Pin and sew, right sides together, leaving a 10-inch opening. Clip seams very carefully around each scallop. Turn right side out and press. Slipstitch the opening closed.

3. Cut three 2-inch lengths of ribbon. Fold one ribbon in thirds by folding each end into the center, overlapping a bit. Turn the ribbon over and sew a button to the middle. Fold another ribbon and sew behind the first at a 60° angle. Fold one more ribbon and sew 120° to the first one. Repeat with more ribbon and buttons to make as many ribboned buttons as there are scallops. Sew a button to the center of each scallop.

❖　　❖　　❖

christmas ball
tree

This sparkling tree makes the perfect centerpiece for a dining table or entrance hall. For the best effect, limit your palette to just one or two colors. We've used new ornaments; however, older balls, found at yard sales and flea markets, will often have a patina that new ones lack. An estate sale yielded the rusty urn used for this base, but you can find aged-looking replicas at craft supply stores—or substitute a small cedar bucket, a galvanized pail with a wooden handle, or a floral china cachepot for the same festive results.

1. Tightly fill the container with a piece of dried floral foam. Squirt glue on one end of the floral stick and insert it into the bottom center of the cone. Then squirt glue on the other end of the stick and push it into the foam in the container, making the bottom of the cone level with the top of the container.

2. Glue an end of the bead garland near the bottom of the cone. Wind the garland around the cone, gluing occasionally to hold it in place, and leaving empty spaces to apply the balls.

3. Attach the balls in a random fashion with straightened ornament hangers pushed into the cone and hot glue. Alternate the size and color of the balls.

MATERIALS

decorative container

dried floral foam

wooden floral stick

Styrofoam cone, about twice the height of the container

Christmas bead garland

large selection of small vintage Christmas balls

wire ornament hangers

TOOLS

hot glue gun and glue sticks

mosaic christmas vase

A favorite piece of china doesn't have to be relegated to the trash heap just because it has shattered into a dozen pieces. This encrusted vase makes use of broken porcelain plates and other china in holiday colors, along with wayward buttons from old clothing and damaged costume jewelry too pretty to throw away. If you don't have anything broken, search for china at thrift shops and yard sales—it doesn't matter if the dishes have chips or stains, since you will be using just bits and pieces. To crack the china easily, use tile nippers (available at hardware stores) instead of just smashing the plate to bits with a hammer.

1. With the putty knife, cover a small area of the container with a layer of adhesive. Press pieces of china, buttons, and jewelry into the adhesive, smoothing the rough, raised cement with your fingers.

2. Continue working around the container in a similar fashion until it is entirely covered. Let dry overnight. Use a razor blade to scrape any dried cement off the pieces of china.

❖   ❖   ❖

MATERIALS

ceramic container

pre-mixed tile adhesive (available in home improvement and hardware stores)

assortment of broken china pieces

buttons, jewelry

TOOLS

small putty knife

razor blade

gingham holiday
teddy bear

This dapper gingham gentleman with a felt vest and velvet bow tie has a cheery stitched face. For Teddy's body, choose a sturdy fabric, but one that's light enough to be easily turned right side out after stitching. We used gingham; a lightweight corduroy would also work. For a floppier effect, fill the bear with beans instead of fiberfill. Our guy is partial to his classic Radio Flyer, but a wooden sleigh or tricycle could just as easily provide transport to his spot under the tree.

1. Using the patterns, cut from the gingham: one body front, one head top, and four ears. From double layers, aligning the checks, cut two body backs, two head sides, two pairs of arms, and two pairs of legs.

2. Stitch the bear together (all stitching is done in 1/4-inch seams, with right sides together):

   For the head, pin and stitch the head sides together, from the nose to the front neck edge. Pin and stitch one edge of the head top to one head side, from the tip of the nose to the back edge. Pin and stitch the other edge of the top to the other head side in the same way. Stitch the back edges of the head sides together. Remove the pins and turn right side out. For the ears, pin and stitch each pair of ears together, leaving the straight edge open. Remove the pins, trim the corners, and turn right side out.

   For the body, pin and stitch the darts on the body front. Pin and stitch the backs together, leaving an opening at the center for stuffing. Pin and stitch the front to the back at the outer edges. Remove the pins and turn right side out.

MATERIALS

1/2 yard gingham cotton and matching thread

about 3/4 pound polyester fiberfill

heavy thread

black embroidery thread

18 inches 1/2-inch-wide velvet ribbon for bow tie

8x15-inch piece green felt and contrasting thread for vest

3 tiny buttons

small piece Velcro

TOOLS

patterns (see page 39)

doll-sculpting needle

embroidery needle

For the arms, match two arm pieces, right sides facing. Pin and stitch together, leaving an opening at the side. Remove the pins and turn right side out. Repeat with the two remaining arm pieces. For the legs, match, pin, and stitch each leg piece in the same way.

3. Stuff all the parts with fiberfill. Slipstitch the openings in the body, arms, and legs closed. Turn the raw edges of the head in $1/4$ inch. Stitch the head to the body. Pucker the ears at the center and stitch to the head. Place the arms on the sides of the body, below the neck and along the seams. With the doll-sculpting needle threaded with heavy thread, push the needle through the body; take a stitch in one arm. Push the needle back through the body; take a stitch through the other arm. Pull the thread tight. Repeat several times. Attach the legs to the base of the body, along the body seams, in the same way.

4. With the embroidery needle and black thread, embroider the eyes, mouth, and nose (or draw on with fabric marker). Tie the ribbon around Teddy's neck, making a bow in front.

5. Using the vest patterns, cut out a double layer of felt for the body and two pockets. Swing a shoulder strap to the back and stitch or glue in place (see pattern). Repeat for the other strap. Using contrasting thread, sew the pockets to the front of the vest. Sew the buttons down the front of one side. Cut a small piece of hook (fuzzy) Velcro and sew to the inside of the same front side.

❖   ❖   ❖

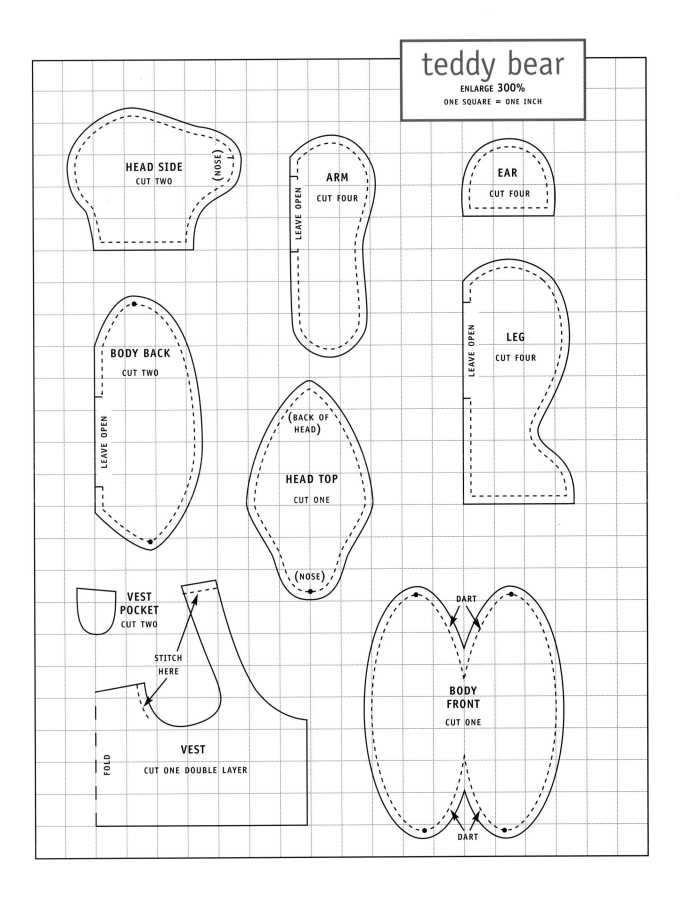

sugared fruit

Arrange these shimmering sugared fruits on a glass epergne for a most elegant centerpiece or to draw attention to a sideboard. Wind satin ribbon through the fruits for further embellishment. If you make these with powdered egg whites, your guests will be able to partake of these little jewels. Try to use an assortment of differently colored and sized fruits, perhaps crabapples, kumquats, lady apples, grapes, oranges, lemons, pomegranates, persimmons, tangelos, and clementines. Sugared fruits should last a few months.

Working with a few pieces of fruit at a time, brush egg white on the fruit. Sprinkle with sugar. Set aside on wire racks to dry for at least 1 hour. Arrange the fruit on a platter or cake stand.

❖ ❖ ❖

MATERIALS

fruit

egg whites, lightly beaten, or equivalent powdered egg whites

granulated sugar

TOOLS

pastry brush

sock snowman

This convention of charming snowmen was fashioned from all manner of disparate materials, including a tot's tube sock, painted papier-mâché globes, and round balls of Styrofoam. Don't skimp on filling the sock snowman—the fatter the better! Shown second from the left in the front row of the photograph opposite, this textured guy is easy to make in multiples. Vary the hat and scarf colors for a cute snowman assembly. Instructions for the other snowmen appear on the following pages.

1. Turn the tube sock inside-out and stuff with fiberfill until full. Gather the sock at the top, pull tight, and sew closed, making the snowman as full as possible.

2. To form the head, wrap a short piece of wire tightly around the snowman one-third down from the toe of the sock. Glue on the buttons to create the face.

3. To make the hat, cut about 4 inches from the top of the ribbed sock. Sew the cut end closed and glue on the pompom. Fold the open end over two times. Place the hat on the head and tack in place.

4. Thread the embroidery needle with a pipe cleaner and use to pull the pipe cleaner through the sides of snowman to make the arms. Twist a small length of pipe cleaner around the end of each arm to make fingers.

5. Fringe the ends of the plaid fabric strip and tie around the snowman's neck.

❖   ❖   ❖

MATERIALS

white toddler-size tube sock and matching thread

polyester fiberfill

white floral wire

buttons

red child-size ribbed sock and matching thread for hat

pompom

black pipe cleaners for arms

8 x 1-inch scrap plaid fabric for scarf

TOOLS

fabric glue

large embroidery needle

salt dough snowmen

These adorable, misshapen snowmen will charm and delight you every year when you pull them out of your Christmas box. One of the squat fellows is shown third from the right on page 42. This easy project is a good one for children to help with. The recipe for the dough makes about six small snowmen.

1. Make the salt dough: Mix the flour and salt in a large bowl. Slowly mix in the warm water with your hands. Knead the dough on a flour-covered surface for about 10 minutes, or until smooth. Keep what you are not using wrapped up or in an airtight container because it dries out quickly.

2. Preheat the oven to 325°F. Roll the dough into balls in two or three different sizes. Stick a toothpick through the center of each ball as a support spine. Stack the balls into snowmen, using two or three for each. Poke holes with a toothpick for faces. Stick toothpicks in the sides for the arms. Put the snowmen on a baking sheet and bake for about 30 minutes, depending on their size, or until they are firm but not too brown. Let them cool completely before painting, about one hour. Paint the snowmen with at least two coats of white paint. Let dry.

3. To make the hats: With the zigzag scissors, make a brim by cutting a circle of black paper to fit proportionally to a snowman's head. Cut a strip of the paper about $1\frac{1}{2}$ inches high and roll into a tube. Tape closed with the double-stick tape. Center and glue it to the hat brim. Cut a small circle to fit the top of the hat and glue it in place. Repeat to make a hat for each snowman.

4. Glue the hats on the heads. Tie a piece of fabric or ribbon around each snowman's neck. Paint black "coal" buttons down their fronts.

❖   ❖   ❖

MATERIALS

salt dough: 4 cups flour, 1 cup salt, and $1\frac{1}{2}$ cups warm water

round toothpicks

white and black acrylic paint

black construction paper

scraps of ribbon and fabric for scarves

TOOLS

paintbrushes

zigzag-edged scissors

straight scissors

double-stick Scotch tape

all-purpose craft glue

styrofoam snowman

An adult should trim the balls to make this snowman (shown at far right on page 42), but as with all of these snowmen projects, children will enjoy choosing and applying the decorations.

1. With the razor blade, slice ⅛ inch off the bottom and top of a medium-size Styrofoam ball. Slice ⅛ inch off the bottom of a small ball. With the white glue, glue the balls together at the sliced-off spots. Let dry. Spray paint the entire snowman white. Let dry.

2. To make the hat, cut a 2-inch circle from the black felt. Cut out a 1-inch center hole from this circle, to make a donut shape. Set aside. With the rubber cement, glue the remaining black felt to the construction paper. For the brim, cut a 2-inch circle from the felt/paper. Cut out a 1-inch center hole from this circle, to make a donut shape. To make the crown, cut a 4 x 1½-inch strip from the felt/paper. Fit the strip into the center hole, scoring the bottom ¼ inch all the way around. Fold the scored flaps onto the paper side of the brim and glue. Glue the 2-inch felt donut to the paper side of the brim. Cut a 1-inch circle from the felt/paper to make the top of the hat and glue in place. Glue the hat to the snowman's head.

3. With the white glue, make the snowman's face by gluing beads, buttons, or other odds and ends to the head. To make the arms, stick pipe cleaners or twigs into the side of the snowman. Cut out four tiny mitten shapes from the red felt. Glue two mittens together around the end of each arm. Tie the gingham strip around his neck for a scarf.

MATERIALS

small and medium Styrofoam balls

floral spray paint (availabe in floral supply stores)

large scrap black felt, at least 8 inches square

construction paper

beads and buttons

pipe cleaners or twigs for arms

scrap red felt for mittens

8 x 1-inch scrap gingham fabric for scarf

TOOLS

razor blade

all-purpose white glue

rubber cement

❖ ❖ ❖

papier-mâché
snowman

Papier-mâché doesn't require a great deal of precision and can be a bit messy, so it's always a fun craft for kids. This snowman, shown at far left in the photo on page 42, will become a treasured keepsake when made by little hands.

1. To make the papier-mâché paste: Bring 2 cups of the water to a boil in a saucepan. Dissolve the flour in the remaining 2 cups cold water. Add the flour mixture to the boiling water. Return to a boil. Add the sugar. Stir and remove from heat to cool and thicken, about 30 minutes.

2. Assemble the snowman: If using Styrofoam balls, put them together in a snowman shape, using toothpicks to hold them in place. If using tin foil (for a more rustic looking snowman), bunch the foil into graduated size balls. Tape them together in the shape of a snowman.

3. Make the snowman's hat by cutting a section of the toilet paper tube 1 to 2 inches long. Use the tube as a pattern to mark a circle on the oak tag for the top of the hat. Cut out. Cut a circle from the oak tag about 3 inches in diameter for the brim. Tape the circles to the tube to form the hat.

4. Cover the snowman and hat with newspaper ripped into 1-inch strips and dipped in the papier-mâché paste. (Remove the excess paste by pulling the strip between two fingers.) Paste on about four layers. Let dry completely, at least 48 hours, on waxed paper or tin foil to insure that shapes do not stick. You may need to turn them so that all sides dry evenly.

5. With the sponge brush, paint all the snowman and hat surfaces with one coat of white paint as a primer. Let dry. Paint the hat black and

MATERIALS

papier-mâché paste: 4 cups cold water, $\frac{1}{2}$ cup flour, and 3 tablespoons sugar

Styrofoam balls of varying sizes, or tin foil

toothpicks

cardboard toilet-paper tube

small piece oak tag

newspaper

white and black acrylic paint

small buttons

pins with colored plastic balls on ends

2 small twigs with forked ends for arms

1 x 7-inch piece red felt, polar fleece, or ribbon for scarf

6-inch square white felt or polar fleece for base

3-inch square cardboard for base

TOOLS

sponge brush

small paintbrush

hot glue gun and glue sticks

the snowman with another coat of white. Decorate with a combination of paint, buttons, and pins to make eyes, nose, mouth, and "coal" buttons.

6. Attach the hat to the top of the snowman's head with hot glue. Glue twigs to the side of the snowman for arms. Cut fringe at either end of the scarf, and tie around the snowman's neck.

7. Cut a wavy edge around the square piece of white felt. Cut a small circle about 1 inch in diameter out of the center. Place the felt on top of the cardboard, with the cut-out circle at center, and glue the snowman to the exposed cardboard circle.

dad and son
snowmen

The jolly father and son at the rear of the photograph on page 42 are made with creamy white wool. If you have the time, it might be fun to create a whole family of snowpeople, including Mom and baby sister. If you're pressed for time this year, why not start a holiday tradition by making just one, and adding a new family member each December? Line them up on a dresser or side table to bring cheer to wintry days. Stitch the faces with black embroidery thread or draw features with a fine-nibbed permanent marker and embellish with tiny beads.

1. Using the dad snowman patterns, cut out two backs, one front, four arms, and one base of white wool. Pin and sew the backs together with a ¼-inch seam allowance, leaving a 2½-inch opening for turning and stuffing. Pin and sew the front to the back with right sides together, ¼-inch seam allowance. Pin and sew on the base circle with right sides together. Turn the snowman right side out. Stuff the body firmly with fiberfill. Slipstitch the back opening closed. Pin and sew two arm pieces together, leaving about 1½ inches open. Repeat to make the second arm. Stuff the arms with fiberfill and slipstitch closed. Slipstitch the arms in position.

2. With the black thread, embroider features on the face. Glue on bead eyes. For the nose, roll the large scrap of orange felt into a cone and trim so the base of the cone is even. Glue in position. Tie the long strip of wool around the snowman's neck for a scarf.

3. To make the dad's hat: Cut a 60 x 2-inch strip of gray felt. Cut out a 5-inch circle of gray felt for the brim. Starting at one end, roll the strip of felt tightly, gluing as you go along. Glue the rolled felt to the center of brim. Cut out a circle of gray felt, the same size as the

MATERIALS

1 ¼ yards white wool or felt and white thread

1 pound polyester fiberfill

black embroidery thread

beads for eyes

2 scraps orange felt for noses: 3 x 3 inches for dad, 2 x 2 inches for boy

2 scraps wool for scarves: 36 x 5 inches for dad, 25 x 2 inches for boy

¼ yard gray felt for dad's hat

sleeve with banded wrist from old sweater for boy's hat and matching thread

pompom for boy's tassel

TOOLS

patterns (see pages 50 and 51)

fabric glue

rolled felt. Glue the circle to the top of the hat. Glue the hat to the dad's head.

4. Repeat Steps 1 and 2 to make the boy snowman.

5. To make the boy's hat: Open the seam of the sweater sleeve. Wrap the wrist around the boy's head to make sure it fits. If it's too big, trim the sleeve at the seam edge. Right sides together, resew the sleeve in a long triangle, coming to a point about 9 inches from the wrist. Trim the seam and turn the hat right side out. Slipstitch the hat to the boy's head. Sew the pompom to the hat's tip.

❖   ❖   ❖

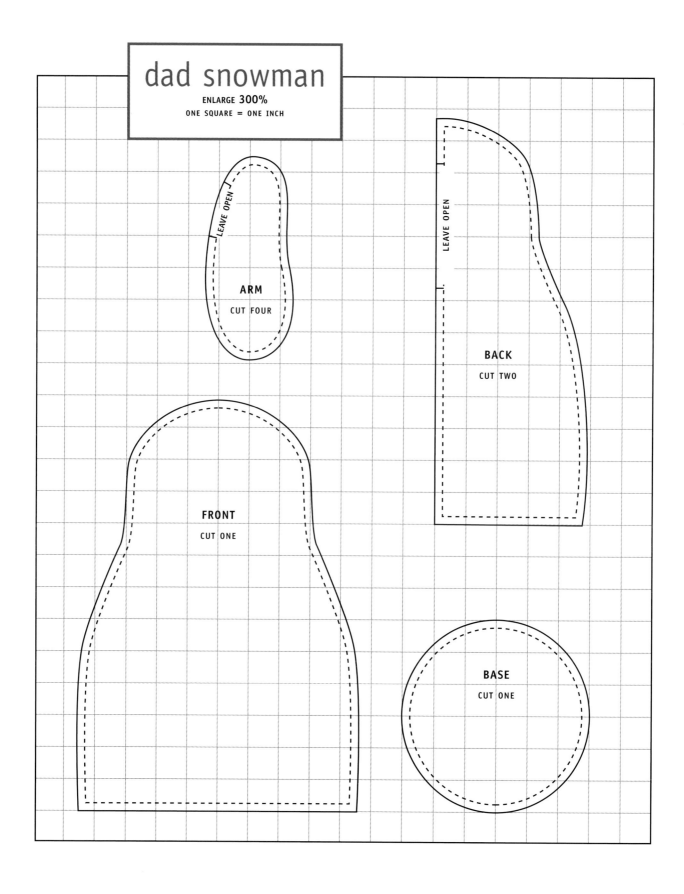

dad snowman

ENLARGE **300%**

ONE SQUARE = ONE INCH

ARM

CUT FOUR

LEAVE OPEN

BACK

CUT TWO

LEAVE OPEN

FRONT

CUT ONE

BASE

CUT ONE

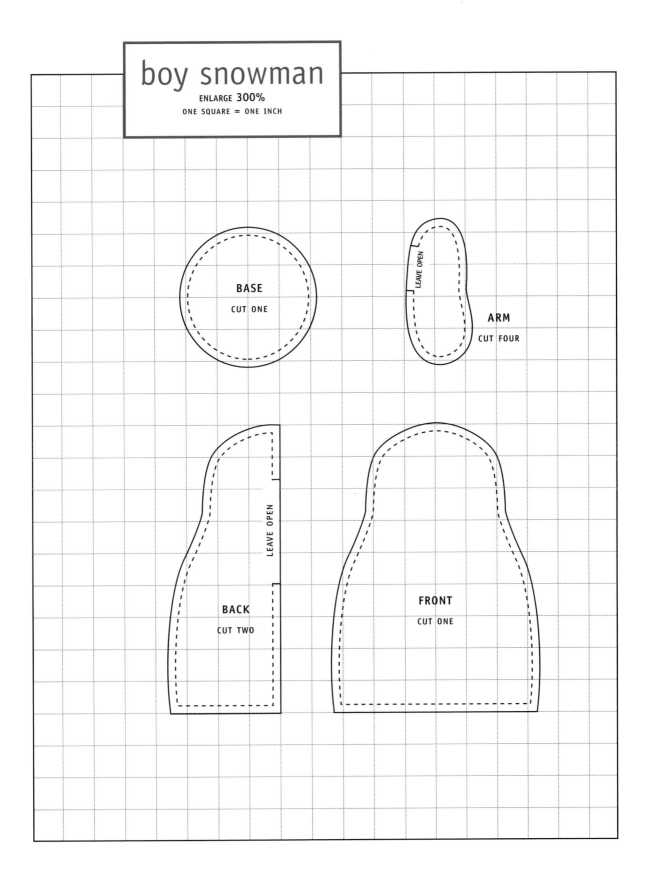

chapter two

trimming
the tree

One of the most beautiful symbols of this season is surely the Christmas **tree**, an ordinary citizen of the woods transformed, for a few weeks, into an undisputed holiday **star**. To spread the spirit everywhere, why not place several trees throughout the house? If your kitchen is large enough, a tree is a fragrant, stately presence in its **native** dress, without any decorations at all. The bedroom is a pretty place for the **gentle** scent and sight of a smaller evergreen, especially at night, with tiny lights twinkling in the dark. A very small tree—perhaps a live sapling—dotted with plaid or raffia **bows** can be a wonderful surprise when tucked in an alcove or nook, or placed on a wide ledge beneath a window.

Small white lights remain the **tree-trimming** standard, although mutilcolored lights are coming back into vogue. Larger colored **bulbs**, circa 1950, and lights with punched-tin reflectors are popular garage-sale finds, and other vintage **ornaments** are so appealing they've spawned collector's clubs across the country.

Cutting down the tree

Chopping down a Christmas tree is a holiday tradition for many families. An afternoon spent combing your own woods or driving to the tree farm and traversing the acreage is an event to remember. Be sure to bring a camera: Your child standing beside the chosen tree, saw in hand, makes an ideal Christmas-card picture.

Measure the height of the room where the tree will stand before you venture out (and don't forget to take the tape measure with you). Choose a tree with a healthy green appearance and flexible needles—avoid trees whose needles cascade down if you run your hand over a branch. To keep your tree fresh for as long as possible, follow these tips from the University of California's Cooperative Extension: Even if your tree is freshly cut, cut another inch off the bottom of the trunk when you get home, before setting the cut end in a bucket of warm water. Leave the tree in the water as it cools overnight, and replace with more warm water the next morning. When that bucket of water has cooled, place the tree in its permanent stand and make sure the water reservoir remains full.

After Christmas, recycle your tree—many communities arrange to collect trees and turn them into chips. Or donate the tree to the birds by placing it in your backyard and strewing bread and suet among the branches.

A living Christmas tree, its roots bound in burlap, can be decorated indoors for the holiday, and planted outside afterward. If you plan to get a living tree, prepare for it in the fall by digging a hole before the ground freezes. Make the hole about two feet deep and fill it with rocks and leaves.

The living tree will be quite happy indoors for a few weeks. Place it in a large sturdy tub or bucket that won't tip. To avoid bruising the roots, cushion the inside of the tub with old towels or newspapers, and steady the trunk in position by stuffing paper between the trunk and the tub. Encase the tub in a festive fabric or top with sheet moss to disguise the root ball.

After Christmas, plant the tree, filling the hole with soil and water. The burlap and twine will disintegrate and so do not need to be removed. Just roll the burlap back if it protrudes from the soil, as it will wick water away from the plant.

A historical legacy

Whether a Christmas tree is decorated or not, it is always the focus of a room. Placing greens inside the house was part of the earliest pagan winter rituals commemorating the end of the harvest. These practices blended, in time, with Christian celebrations, and the results are the Christmas trees and garlands we decorate with today.

In Europe, an undecorated evergreen tree, or yule tree, was traditionally planted outdoors to mark the winter solstice. Eventually, Christian missionaries moved the tree inside as a symbol of life through the long cold winter. The Germans decorated their trees with small white wafers, cookies, pastries, and cakes, and, eventually, lights and ornaments. Legend holds that Hessian soldiers brought the first Christmas tree to the American colonies during the Revolutionary War, although the practice of decorating a tree did not spread until the 19th century. Queen Victoria's German husband, Prince Albert of Saxony, set up a tree at Windsor Castle in 1841, popularizing the concept in England.

Coating trees, inside and out

An indoor tree will look like it's been covered with fresh-fallen snow when you follow this simple recipe: In a very large bowl, mix up a batter of 1½ cups snowy soap flakes (such as Ivory Snow) and 4 to 6 cups boiling water added slowly. Beat with a mixer until very fluffy. String lights on the tree before applying the snow, and protect the floor with a plastic drop cloth. Apply the mixture to the tree branches with a stiff paintbrush or rubber-gloved hands. Let dry overnight. Two cups soap and ½ cup water makes a craft dough for tabletop snowmen.

christmas greenery

The most common holiday trees are pine, fir, spruce, cedar, and cypress.

The Scotch pine has short, stiff, bundled needles with a bluish cast, and a typical "Christmas tree" appearance. Fir trees have upright cones and two rows of short, stiff, flat needles on each branch. Spruce trees such as the blue spruce (also known as a Colorado spruce) look similar to fir trees, but their needles are round, not flat. They have hanging cones, blue-green pointed needles that spiral around each branch, and a Christmas tree shape and scent. Their long branches often sweep to the ground. Cedar and cypress trees have sharp, prickly, clustered needles that get scaly when the trees are older. Greens from all of these trees can be shaped into wreaths, mixed with boxwood, holly, ivy, or juniper.

And don't forget the mistletoe, which comes from a shrub and is the prime ingredient in a kissing ball, traditionally hung in an entryway as a mainstay of Christmas romance. Handle mistletoe carefully; it is toxic if ingested by people or pets. *(Information courtesy of University of Georgia, College of Architectural and Environmental Sciences, at www.bugwood.caes.uga.edu)*

Outdoors, near a window and some protective shrubbery, decorate a feed-the-birds tree. Anchor a small cut evergreen in a mound of snow. Coat the branches with a feeding mix made of 3 cups of melted suet or fat mixed with 2 cups of dry ingredients, including cornmeal, sugar, berries, oatmeal, and bird seed such as millet and sunflower seeds. Adjust the proportions as necessary to create the proper consistency. Generally, the amount of suet will be one and a half times greater than the amount of dry ingredients.

Tree skirts

A skirt gives your tree a party air, framing it from below and balancing the ornaments above. It has practical applications, too: It gives presents something to rest on instead of the floor, catches falling pine needles, and covers an unsightly tree-holder. A country quilt (use a slightly damaged one, as pine resin might drip onto it) makes a marvelous tree skirt, folded diagonally and wrapped around the tree like a bandana. A lace tablecloth or a large piece of felt has the same effect, and so does a fancy velvet or taffeta party skirt found at a thrift shop and put to new use.

A time-honored ritual continues when a freshly cut pine comes home for the holidays, strapped to the top of the family van.

A gift of an ornament

There's nothing more thoughtful than a gift crafted by hand, and ornaments created by the giver are especially heartwarming. Make ornaments using pre-cut wooden shapes bought at a crafts shop, or cut them yourself. Embellish ordinary colored balls with glue, glitter, and curlicues, or use paint pens to write the names of family members on them, accompanied by stamp-size photographs. Stuff clear balls with lavender seeds or other colorful small botanicals, tinsel, or holiday confetti by removing the ornament holder on top and inserting the decorations with tweezers. Look around consignment stores for small treasures—an antique calling card case, a pocket watch—that a chain or ribbon could transform into a hanging ornament.

For a newborn, make a "Baby's First Christmas" ornament that includes the little one's name and the year. In fact, whenever you give or receive an ornament, it's a good idea to write the date and giver's name on the back or bottom with a thin-pointed indelible marker. This way, tree trimming will be accompanied by, "Remember when . . . ." instead of, "Who gave us . . . ?"

A special Christmas—the first one together for a married couple, perhaps—might be marked by the gift of a vintage ornament. The first ornaments were made in the early 1800s by German glassblowers; F. W. Woolworth imported them to the United States in 1880. Larger ornaments are considered more collectible than smaller ones; those with cracks or missing paint hold little monetary value. And while in general the more unusual the design, the more valuable, this is not true for Santa Claus, who remains the most sought-after form.

Storing decorations

Keep decorations in their original packaging whenever possible—if the packaging begins to show wear, put the ornaments inside a large, sturdy box. Or wrap ornaments individually in tissue paper and stack them gently in a box padded with newspapers. Tiny ornaments can be kept in an egg carton or a compartmentalized plastic box—the kind used to organize embroidery floss or beads. However you do it, at the end of the season label your boxes descriptively. Each year, as I search for a particular holiday something, I'm reminded that the label "Christmas stuff," though honest, doesn't really help. Well-marked boxes allow you to unearth the Advent calendar before Advent ends and put your hands on the To-From tags left over from last year before you buy hundreds more.

Because this tall wispy tree has lacy see-through foliage, a collection of handblown ornaments and garlands is shown off to perfection. The entry-hall location ensures the tree gets maximum attention.

christmas
potpourri

In the summer, collect fragrant roses and lavender and hang them upside down in a dark, cool place to dry; then save to fill these potpourri pouches. Come the yuletide, set the fragrant bundles on a decorative plate to fill the air with their lovely scent. The same spices could also be mixed with a combination of green pine needles, small pinecones, and rose hips for a woodsier aroma. Make a number of smaller sachets and hang them from the tree for double-duty ornaments, as shown in the photograph on page 10.

Combine the rose petals, lavender, allspice, cinnamon, orrisroot, cloves, and rose oil in the container. Seal and set aside six weeks. Surround a portion of the potpourri with a double layer of tulle. Gather the corners together and tie with a long length of ribbon threaded with an ornament.

❖   ❖   ❖

MATERIALS

8 cups dried rose petals

1 cup dried lavender flowers

2 tablespoons ground allspice

2 tablespoons ground cinnamon

2 tablespoons ground orrisroot

1 tablespoon ground cloves

4 drops rose oil

squares of tulle in assorted colors

ribbon or string

miniature ornaments

TOOLS

airtight container

angel cookies

Hanging from the tree, or arranged on a Christmas platter ready for little (and big) hands to grab, these heaven-sent cookies are pleasing to the eye and the palate.

1. In a large bowl with an electric mixer on medium speed, beat the butter and shortening until well blended; add the granulated sugar and beat until light. Add the eggs, one at a time, beating well after each addition.

2. In a medium-size bowl, combine the flour, baking powder, and salt. With the mixer on low, add half of the flour mixture to the butter mixture and beat just until blended; add the remaining flour mixture and beat until a soft dough forms. Shape the dough into three equal balls; wrap and refrigerate at least 30 minutes.

3. To cut and bake the cookies: Heat the oven to 350°F. Lightly grease two baking sheets. Cut two pieces of waxed paper the same size as the baking sheets. Lightly flour the waxed paper and roll out one ball of dough between the paper to $1/8$-inch thickness. Remove the top piece of waxed paper. With angel cookie cutters, cut out as many angels as possible from the dough, leaving $1/2$ inch between the cookies. Remove all the trimmings and press together. Invert the waxed paper with the angels onto a greased baking sheet and peel off the waxed paper. Reroll the trimmings between waxed paper and repeat cutting and inverting angels to fill the second baking sheet. If making cookies for ornaments, use a small straw or toothpick to pierce a small hole about $1/2$ inch from the top of each cookie.

1/2 cup (1 stick) butter

1/4 cup vegetable shortening

1 1/3 cups granulated sugar

2 large eggs

3 1/2 cups unsifted all-purpose flour

1/2 teaspoon baking powder

1/2 teaspoon salt

2 1-pound packages confectioners' sugar

6 large egg whites or equivalent powdered egg whites

1 teaspoon cream of tartar

yellow food coloring

small gold dragées (optional)

4. Bake the cookies 8 to 10 minutes, or until golden. Cool 4 minutes on the baking sheets, then remove to wire racks and cool completely before decorating. Repeat rolling, cutting, and baking with the remaining balls of dough and trimmings.

5. To make royal icing: In a large bowl with an electric mixer on low speed, beat the confectioners' sugar, egg whites, and cream of tartar until mixed. Increase the speed to high, and beat until very thick and fluffy, about 6 minutes. Cover tightly with plastic wrap to prevent drying until ready to use.

6. To decorate the cookies: Divide the icing between two bowls. Cover one bowl tightly with plastic wrap. Using just a few drops of yellow food coloring, tint the other bowl of icing a very pale yellow. With a pastry brush, paint the front of each cookie with a thin coating of tinted icing, being sure not to cover the pierced hole; let dry and paint again. Let dry. Pipe decorative designs on the front of the cookies using the reserved white icing and a pastry bag fitted with a small (#1) writing tip. If using small gold dragées, place on cookies before the icing dries. If making cookies well in advance, store in an airtight container and freeze.

MAKES ABOUT 3 DOZEN 6-INCH COOKIES

❖   ❖   ❖

Star-shaped cutters inspired by classic patchwork-quilt patterns were used to cut these cookies for decorating a tree. The cookies were brushed with white icing and highlighted with touches of liquid silver or a sprinkling of silver dragées, available at cake-decorating stores.

rustic twig stars

Sometimes the humblest materials make the most delightful seasonal adornments. These stars were fashioned from twigs gathered in the backyard and bound with bits of twine and fabric. As a variation, make simple house shapes or let the curve of the twigs inspire you to other creations.

1. Break twigs into pieces about 5 inches in length.

2. With a ruler and pencil, draw a star on a piece of waxed paper, making each line 5 inches long. Using the pattern as a guide, glue the twigs together with hot glue.

3. Wrap a piece of twine or thin, ripped strips of fabric around four of the five points several times and tie in a small knot. Through the fifth point, tie a loop of twine for the star to hang, and then wrap the point, securing the loop to the top of the point as you tie it.

❖   ❖   ❖

MATERIALS

twigs in various sizes

twine and fabric scraps

TOOLS

waxed paper

hot glue gun and glue sticks

papier-mâché ornaments

Almost any paper or cloth odds-and-ends can transform simple papier-mâché balls into special mementos. If you mark the ornament with the date, you'll preserve the memory of making it for years to come. Use pinking shears when cutting up ribbons and fabrics to keep them from fraying.

1. To make the papier-mâché paste: Bring 2 cups of the water to boil in a saucepan. Dissolve the flour in the remaining 2 cups cold water. Add the flour mixture to the boiling water. Return to a boil. Add the sugar. Stir and remove from the heat to cool and thicken, about 30 minutes.

2. Cover the balloons with newspaper ripped into 1-inch strips and dipped in the papier-mâché paste. (Remove excess paste by pulling the strip between two fingers.) Apply strips to all sides of the balloons, until about four layers have been applied, leaving a small gap around the knot at the top of the balloon. Let dry completely, at least 48 hours, on waxed paper or tin foil so that the balloons do not stick. You may need to turn them so that all sides dry evenly.

3. Pop the balloons by sticking a pin into the tops, near the knot. Remove the balloons. With a sponge brush, paint the balls with one coat of white paint as a primer. Let dry. Apply two coats of red or green paint, letting the paint dry between coats.

4. Apply decorations. Here are some ideas:

   Make pretty snowflakes by folding 2-inch squares and circles of white paper in half, then in quarters, then in eighths. Cut various holes and shapes into the edges. Unfold. Attach the snowflakes to a ball with Mod Podge.

MATERIALS

papier-mâché paste: 4 cups cold water, $1/2$ cup flour, and 3 tablespoons sugar

balloons blown to 4- or 5-inch diameters

newspaper

white, red, and green acrylic paint

things to decorate balls, such as: construction paper, ribbon scraps, white cotton twine, color copies of photos, sticker dots

Mod Podge

large paper clips

buttons at least $3/4$ inch in diameter

TOOLS

sponge brushes

pinking shears

decorative-edged scissors

small paintbrush

wire cutters

small pliers

hot glue gun and glue sticks

Cut small scraps of Christmas ribbons into 1-inch squares with the pinking shears. Apply to the ball with Mod Podge in a checkerboard pattern, leaving blank spaces between the squares.

Starting at the hole at the top of the ball, attach white cotton twine in a spiral pattern, about 2 inches at a time, with glue or Mod Podge, holding the twine in place until it sticks before moving on.

Color photocopy pictures of friends or family so that the image of their face is approximately 1 inch square. Mount on top of a larger square of white paper and trim with decorative scissors. Attach to the ball with Mod Podge. Add funny hats made of construction paper with hole punches for pompoms.

Apply sticker dots of different sizes to the surface of the ball.

5. Paint the year on the bottom of the ball with a small paint brush and a complementary paint color. Let dry. Apply one coat of Mod Podge to the entire surface of ball with a sponge brush. Let dry.

6. To make a hook, with the wire cutters cut a large paper clip into two "U" shapes. Thread one U-shaped wire through two holes of a button so that the ends come through on the bottom side of the button. Bend the two ends of the paper clip outward slightly with pliers so that it will not come unthreaded, and so that the ends of the paper clip can still be inserted into the hole in the top of the ball. Push the ends of the paper clip into the top of ball, covering the hole with the button. Secure with hot glue. Thread a short length of ribbon through the hook and tie in a bow. Repeat to attach hooks to all the ornaments.

❖   ❖   ❖

felted wool
ornaments

These ornaments don't have to hang on the tree, nor do they need to be put away with the other Christmas ornaments. They are quite at home in a variety of places around the house and they add warmth and spirit to just about any room all year 'round. Hang them in windows, from the mantel, on a Shaker peg rack in the bathroom, or on a doorknob. For fragrant ornaments, fill each one with a bit of potpourri or star anise before sewing the seams together.

▲ To make the checkerboard ornament: Cut red and green felted wool into $1/2$-inch-wide strips. Butt the edges of the strips next to each other, alternating green and red. Machine sew them together with a zigzag stitch, until you have made a large, striped square. Press with a hot iron. Cut this piece into $1/2$-inch-wide strips, cutting perpendicular to the stripes, so that each strip contains alternating blocks of color. Rearrange the strips, offsetting each by one square, so they form a checkerboard pattern. Sew the strips to each other, using the zigzag stitch. Press with a hot iron.

To make a pattern, draw a design of your choice (star, heart, etc.) on a piece of paper and cut out. Use the pattern to cut the design out of the checkerboard piece of felt. Cut the same design, only slightly larger, out of a solid piece of wool.

Cut a 12-inch length of twine. Lay the checkerboard piece on top of the solid piece of wool, with the ends of the twine piece inserted between the two layers, creating a loop. Pin in place. Machine stitch the layers together, using a zigzag stitch along the edge. Remove the pins.

Cut around the perimeter of the ornament. Leave a slight amount of the backing to show around the edge and be careful not to cut

MATERIALS

felted wool made from sweaters (see page 75 for instructions for making felted wool) and matching thread

twine

buttons

through the edge-stitching and the twine loop. Decorate with one or more buttons.

You can also make a checkerboard pattern with more than two colors of wool, like in our heart ornament. Arrange wool strips of three of four different colors in a random pattern and sew together. Cut the piece into strips going the other way. Then offset the strips by one, two, or three blocks (play around with the patterns you can create), and sew back together.

▲ To make the patchwork ornament: Butt the edges of different size pieces of felted wool together to make a large patchwork piece. Machine sew them together with a zigzag stitch, using different colors of thread. Press with a hot iron. Complete the ornament as directed for the checkerboard ornament.

❖   ❖   ❖

felted wool

Felted wool can be made from old sweaters, blankets, and other wool items. When wool is subjected to heat, soap, and agitation, the fibers shrink and form a dense piece of felt. Like store-bought felt, the fabric does not need hems.

▲ Choose old sweaters or blankets that are 100 percent wool. Wool that is labeled "washable" will not shrink. Wash similar colors together since dyes may bleed.

▲ Wash the wool pieces with detergent and hot water several times on the roughest agitation cycle your machine has. Once the sweaters have gone through three or four wash cycles, they will be as felted as they are likely to get. Keep in mind that different kinds of wool will felt differently, some more than others.

▲ Dry the wool on the dryer's hot setting. Cut open the seams and steam-iron the fabric to create flat pieces of felt wool.

wool-scrap garland

A cheerful, out-of-the-ordinary garland can be made from small squares of bright felted wool snaked onto heavyweight thread and anchored with a button at either end. An alternative to the felted wool would be to use spongy, lofty fabrics such as fleece or felt, which are thick but easy to thread. Insert buttons and jingle bells at intervals to add bright color and sound. Display this garland anywhere you'd like to add a bit of cheer: draped over the back of a chair, mirror, or black-and-white framed photograph, swagged from a doorway, or entwined in a chandelier.

1. Cut the felted wool into small pieces, about 1 or 2 inches square. Keep the pieces generally the same but do not attempt to cut all of them exactly the same. Irregularity of shape and size add to the garland's appeal.

2. Cut a 10-foot piece of thread. Thread a needle, doubling the thread but not knotting it. Thread the string through two holes of a button, creating a 3-inch loop for hanging, and knot the thread on both sides of the button for security.

3. String 20 to 25 pieces of felt, then about 10 buttons, a bell, then another 10 buttons. Repeat with more felt, buttons, and bell. End with a section of felt scraps and a button when you reach about 3 feet in length. Double back and anchor your thread through the button to the last piece of felt, forming a hanging loop as you do so.

❖   ❖   ❖

MATERIALS

felted wool made from sweaters, in a variety of colors (see page 75 for instructions for making felted wool)

string or heavy yarn

buttons of varying colors and sizes (choose buttons with fairly large buttonholes)

bells

TOOLS

needle large enough to hold the string, yet small enough to go through the buttonholes

felted wool
stocking

The tradition of hanging stockings dates back to the legend of Saint Nicholas, who is said to have thrown coins down the chimneys of poor, but deserving, peasants on Christmas Eve. If you don't have a chimney, hang your stockings from the children's bedposts, the side of a staircase, the or, as here, from a cupboard in the dining room. Below are the instructions for making the felted wool stocking at left in the photograph; the instructions for the covered-button stocking are on the following page. Both of these stockings have ribbon loops for hanging; you might try suspending them from the weighted metal holders made to hang stockings from a mantelpiece or table.

1. Using the pattern, cut out the front and back of the stocking from the wool felt. (If there is ribbing at the bottom of the sweater, be careful not to cut into it.) Sew the two pieces together with the tapestry thread, using a blanket stitch.

2. Cut a $17 \times 3\frac{1}{2}$-inch cuff from the sweater, including the bottom ribbing of the sweater, if there is one. Wrap the cuff around the top of the stocking, overlapping the ends of the cuff at the front. Sew the cuff to the stocking at the top, using a blanket stitch. Also use a blanket stitch to finish the exposed end of the cuff. Sew the buttons to the cuff.

3. Use a length of wool piping or cut a strip from the wool to make a hanging loop. Fold in half and sew the two ends just inside the stocking top on the left side.

❖　　❖　　❖

MATERIALS

felted wool sweater in seasonal colors (see page 75 for instructions for making felted wool)

wool tapestry thread

2 large buttons

wool piping

TOOLS

pattern (see page 81)

covered-button
stocking

This green felt stocking patterned with felt- and corduroy-covered buttons is lively enough to claim Santa's full attention. Working with felt guarantees the simplicity of this project, because it is so easy to work with; just sew the seams and trim with pinking shears. Metal buttons with removable backs are specially pronged to hold a fabric covering in place. A wide velvet ribbon is a quick way to decorate the cuff, or use a piece of velvet fabric instead.

1. Using the pattern, cut out the front and back of the stocking from green felt. Sew the two pieces together along the stitch line. Trim the edges with the pinking shears.

2. To make the cuff, cut a strip of felt 15 x 4 inches. Turn the top edge under ½ inch and press with a hot iron. Trim the bottom edge with the pinking shears. Center the 2-inch ribbon on the cuff and glue in place, stitching the ends together in back.

3. Position the cuff on the stocking, placing the top edge of the stocking just below the folded edge of the cuff. Glue the cuff in position.

4. Follow the package instructions for covering the buttons. Glue or sew the buttons to the front of the stocking. To make a loop for hanging, fold the ¾-inch ribbon in half lengthwise, velvet side out, and press with a hot iron. Sew the two ends just inside the stocking top on the left side.

❖   ❖   ❖

MATERIALS

¾ yard green felt and matching thread

15 inches 2-inch-wide velvet ribbon

12 button forms for fabric-covered buttons, in assorted sizes

fabric for covering buttons

5 inches ¾-inch-wide velvet ribbon

TOOLS

pattern (see opposite)

pinking shears

fabric glue

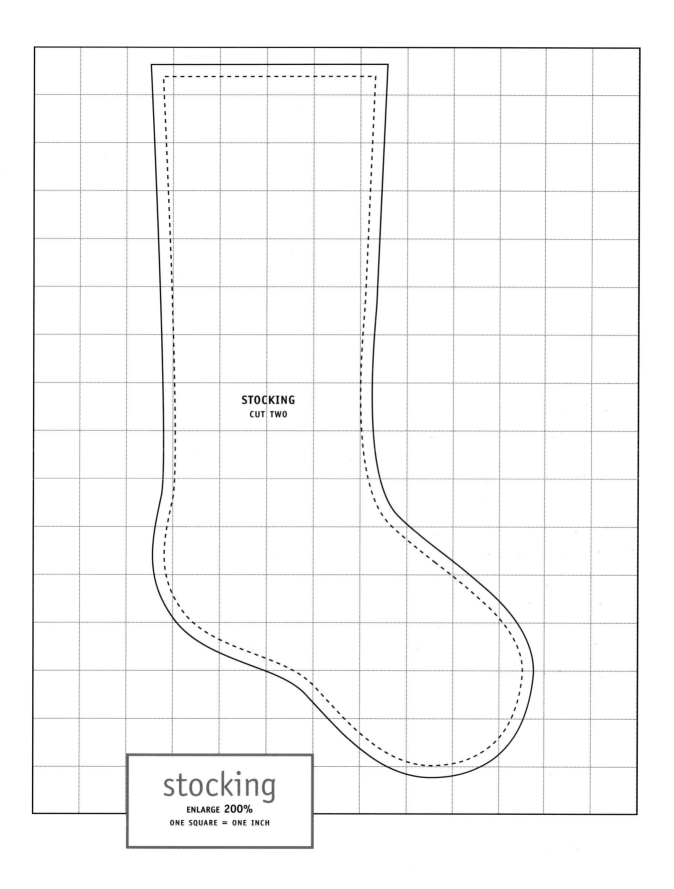

STOCKING
CUT TWO

stocking

ENLARGE 200%
ONE SQUARE = ONE INCH

chapter three

the well-dressed gift

A **beautifully** wrapped present and a sincerely composed card always express the giver's thoughtfulness and creativity. In these days of mass-produced sentiments, handmade, personalized cards and gift wrap are especially **meaningful** and festive. Making cards, tags, and wrappings is a good way to get into the spirit of the season, too, so pick an afternoon early in December to set up your own "Santa's workshop."

The perfect wrapping should convey a **mood** through its color and style, whether the efforts are Zen-like and simple or wonderfully elaborate. Like the gift itself, the best gift wraps reveal time spent and **attention** paid. But not all gifts require a paper wrapping: Some "wrappings" have a life of their own after the gift has been "opened." The perfect presentation piece for your gift might be a pottery bowl or enamel cup, a china plate or platter, glassware or a compote. If you're bringing gifts for a crowd, place them in a wooden crate **decorated** with sprigs of pine and candy canes. Wrapping gifts in a vintage napkin or scarf, a personalized pillowcase, or a blanket-stitched piece of thermal fleece not only doubles your gift but makes an inventive showing.

Many objects with the most practical of applications can become attractive holders for gifts. During the year, collect apple baskets, green plastic or balsa wood strawberry baskets, clementine boxes, jars, tin baking molds, wooden cheese boxes, and flower pots, and bring them back to life at Christmas. Often all that is needed to embellish these containers is a wide ribbon, a bit of greenery, or perhaps some gingham fabric to line the inside. These are particularly nice when they tie to the gift in some way—an assortment of gourmet cooking tools set in a large mason jar, for example, or gardening tools rising out of a glazed flower pot.

Paper wrappings

Inventive wrap can be fashioned from all sorts of everyday items: Give a second look to blueprints, vintage wallpaper scraps, posters, children's artwork, pages from glossy magazines, and maps for quick, one-of-a-kind gift wrappings. There are many kinds of papers available at stationery, hardware, and art supply stores that aren't necessarily made for giftwrapping but serve the purpose well—materials such as shelf paper, wallpaper, kraft paper (use the lightweight kind, not the heavier

shipping paper), coated finger-painting paper, freezer paper, and the no-seam paper used for bulletin boards.

The plainest wrapping paper comes alive when you decorate it with patterns created with rubber stamps and multicolored ink pads, cut-potato stamps, stickers, or colored pens and pencils. Experiment with designs. If you're working with rubber stamps, for example, use a mix of very large and very small stamps to give variety to this craft. For a shimmery effect that's perfect for holiday greeting cards and wrappings, dust a rubber-stamped image with glitter-like embossing powder when it's still wet. Work with a plain piece of paper beneath you to catch the excess powder so you can pour it back into the bottle for re-use. Warming the embossed image over a heat source like a light bulb or toaster melts the powder into permanence. Stamps shaped like angels, cherubs, Christmas trees, or snowmen are particularly amenable to this sparkly treatment.

Alternatively, dip stamps in silver or gold paint and press them repeatedly across matte wrapping paper. For a layered effect, press a gold stamp on top of a silver stamp, or vice versa, letting each stamp dry between coats.

Holiday-motif papers abound, but the classic solid colors have an enduring appeal: shiny reds, greens, and golds. Also keep on hand plenty of colored tissue, and cellophane printed with stars or in lollipop colors to wrap around boxless gifts.

The ribbon

The secret to a well-wrapped present is lots of ribbon, proclaims one inveterate gift-giver, and who would disagree? Ribbons are truly the icing on the cake. They make any present more festive and fun. Consider almost any long, trailing object as potential ribbon and you'll unlock the fastening possibilities in measuring tapes, embroidery floss, raffia, red bakery string, frizzy hemp, lengths of printed camp nametags, bronzed wire, lanyards, and colored thread. For a bit of whimsy, bind a gift with shoelaces, a jump rope, or plastic banner tape from the hardware store that says CAUTION or DO NOT CROSS.

Within the world of "true" ribbons, there are many choices. Grosgrain ribbon, which is a ribbed woven ribbon, was traditionally used by milliners to decorate hats and bonnets. It adds a nice texture to a wrapped gift. The gloss of satin ribbon makes it a popular choice for gift wrapping—it is available as single-face, which is shiny on one side only, or the more expensive double-face, with two shiny sides. Wired ribbon, which has very thin wire embedded along both outside edges, has the unique ability to be bent and shaped for a

three-dimensional effect. Some of the prettiest wired ribbons are imported from France, and are shaded horizontally from dark to light. Curling ribbon is classic: the more of it, the better. It can cascade around a gift or be balled up into a buoyant pompom. And velvet ribbon is always a luxury.

Express your personal style

Are you classic? Inventive? In love with the color purple? Whatever your passion is, express it in your gift wrappings. Golds, reds, and deep forest greens convey the spirit of the Wise Men carrying gold, frankincense, and myrrh. Stripes, plaids, and gingham checks express an exuberant mood. Likewise, show your spirit through the greeting cards you make (see projects, pages 103 and 105) or the photographs you choose to share with others. Sending a casual black-and-white picture of the family on the beach, a formal color portrait of the kids in their holiday best, or a snapshot of man's best friend in front of the Christmas tree might be the perfect expression of you.

Setting up a gift wrap center

Think of a gift wrap center as a luxury you can't afford not to have. Here you can wrap gifts and get them ready for mailing. Indeed, if you set aside an area for all of your projects at Christmas time, including wrapping, you will be able to leave projects temporarily without subjecting others in the house to the turmoil. You'll need a big long table (a board or door on sawhorses would work, too). Stock it with all your supplies, including the things you'll need for shipping—wrapping paper, scissors, tape, brown mailing paper, parcel tape, mailing labels, and stamps. Nest empty packing boxes of various sizes underneath so they are easy to reach. Thread rolls of ribbon on heavy string stretched between two hooks or nails, and rig a big roll of wrapping paper the same way. If you have lots of different papers, arrange them (like flowers in a vase) in a tall garbage can or umbrella stand. Call the post office or UPS for a pickup at home if you have many presents to mail at once.

Gift boxes

A hatbox or shoe box can hold one large gift or—more intriguingly—several little gifts. A simple wooden box from a craft shop can be spruced up in a number of different ways: Sponge-paint by dipping a cut piece of sponge into paint and dabbing it on the box. Spatter-paint by rubbing a toothbrush across a paint-laden comb over the box, or comb-paint a freshly painted surface by wriggling a rubber comb through the wet paint. Decoupage a box with tissue paper, photographs, illustrations from an old garden book, elegant

European candy wrappers, pictures from fashion or garden catalogs, or handmade paper from an art supply store. Boxes can also be surfaced with pearl buttons or small mosaic tiles, either whole or broken into shapes with tile nippers. Press transfer type on a plain white box, or cover it with felt. Gluing miniature or doll-size silverware, cups, and saucers on top of a round Shaker box makes a nice tableau; inside, hide a food-related gift.

Perhaps because we think they might contain something for us, a display of boxes can be an eye-catching Christmas decoration. Stack pretty hatboxes in graduated sizes and tie them with a diaphanous organdy ribbon—no one else needs to know the boxes are empty inside!

Gift bags

The tantalizing tease of a see-through bag makes any gift irresistible. Tucking a tiny present in a cellophane bag with colored crimped paper (crinkle shred) and a pretty bow or metallic twist-tie is fast and easy, and makes the most of something small. Find cellophane bags at craft or party stores, or at sweet shops that sell candy-making supplies. To cover a large gift basket quickly, slip it into a clear or colored cellophane shrink-wrap bag, and warm it with a hair dryer to activate the shrink.

Solid-color gift bags are a familiar and favorite quick-wrap; just drop in your present with a sheet of tissue paper, and you're done! To personalize your present, stencil the bag or cover it with holiday stickers or magazine cutouts that hew to a theme. Attach a holiday gift card to the handle of the bag using a hole punch and thin gold cord or jaunty plaid ribbon. Secure the tissue paper around the gift with a pretty sticker or gold notary stamp.

To make your own gift bag, use a stack of books as a mold, wrapping mid-weight paper around the books, taping the seams of the bag, and then removing the books. Thread yarn or twine through holes punched at the top of the bag, or tie the bag closed with ribbon.

Gift tags

Making gift tags from old Christmas cards is a time-tested way to recycle. Cut the cards with decorative-edged scissors, which cut with a wavy or scalloped edge. A deckle-edge gives any cutout the look of an old-time photograph. (These tags make pretty ornaments for the tree, as well.) Gift tags can also be made from luggage tags, store-bought or cut out of colored oak tag or cardstock and decorated with rubber stamps or stencils. Luggage tags are large enough to hold both a message and a design. Make tags that feature the recipient—scan and print out a picture of them from the computer, or make a small-scale photocopy,

and attach it to cardstock. Start making gift tags a few months before the holiday, or even on summer vacation, when you have the time and energy to focus on small touches.

Displaying cards

Put your Christmas cards in a big wooden sleigh on the floor, or in a shallow basket on an entryway table or by the fireplace so that everyone in the family can read through them. Tape cards to the balusters of a staircase and around mirrors, or stand the prettiest ones on end in the windows so they're right at eye level. There are decorative double-faced tapes that look like wallpaper borders specially made to display your Christmas cards, and the Christmas card clothesline remains a holiday standard. Holiday ribbons make pretty displays for the cards (see project, page 89). However you display them, make your Christmas cards part of your holiday decor.

gift toppers

Little extras make a gift come alive. Lollipops and candy canes are always a good choice for children, and so are pretty pencils, a little toy or whistle, a cinnamon stick, or a bubble wand and suds. Similarly, presents can be decorated with feathers, buttons, charms, starfish, and beads.

HAPPY HOLIDAYS

festive card holders

Show off your favorite Christmas cards on easy-to-make display ribbons. Hang the layered ribbons from the back of a door, as pictured here, or attach them to a wall in a hallway or kitchen—wherever people tend to congregate. For an ever-changing display, replace older cards with newer ones as they arrive in the weeks before Christmas.

1. Cut a length of the 5-inch plaid ribbon and the 2½-inch grosgrain ribbon to fit the height of the door you will hang the card holders on, about 80 inches. Center the grosgrain ribbon on the plaid ribbon. Sew across one end, securing the two ribbons together.

2. Cut the ⅛-inch satin ribbon into 8-inch lengths, as many as the number of cards you will be hanging. Attach a length of this ribbon to a clip by looping it around the clip part of the wire. Leave two equidistant strands of ribbon to hang from a button. Hand sew each clip to the grosgrain ribbon, sewing through to the plaid ribbon. Make sure the loose strands of the satin ribbon extend upward.

3. With the glue gun, glue the loose ends of the satin ribbon to the back of a button, so that it appears as if the clip is hanging from the button. Glue the button to the grosgrain ribbon. Repeat for each clip, alternating button sizes and positioning them on the ribbon a comfortable card-length apart. Center and glue down three small buttons in a triangular pattern to finish off the bottom of the ribbon. Cut a triangle out of the bottom ends of the ribbon with the pinking shears for a decorative finish.

MATERIALS

3 yards 5-inch-wide plaid wire ribbon

7½ yards 2½-inch-wide grosgrain ribbon and matching thread

⅛-inch-wide satin ribbon

square wire "holding" clips (not paper clips; available in office supply stores)

buttons in various sizes

5½ yards 1½-inch-wide check ribbon

TOOLS

hot glue gun and glue sticks

pinking shears

flat-head thumbtacks

4. To make the two smaller cardholders, cut two door-length pieces of the 2 1/2-inch grosgrain ribbon and two of the 1 1/2-inch check ribbon. For each holder, center the check ribbon on the grosgrain ribbon and sew across one end. Repeat Steps 2 and 3 to make two more card holders.

5. To create a large bow-tie style bow, cut an 18-inch length of the 5 1/2-inch plaid ribbon, a 4-inch length of the 2 1/2-inch grosgrain ribbon, and a 4-inch length of the 1 1/2-inch check ribbon. Fold the plaid ribbon in thirds by folding each end into the center, overlapping a bit. Gather in the center and secure with wire. Wrap the grosgrain and check ribbon around the gathered center and secure with fabric glue.

6. To make a smaller bow, use one 12-inch length of grosgrain ribbon, one 12-inch length of check ribbon, and one 3-inch length of check ribbon.

7. Secure the finished bows with fabric glue near the top of the card holders. Hang the holders from the top of the door with thumbtacks.

❖   ❖   ❖

These beautiful old boxes have a faded grandeur that should not be hidden under gift wrap. The simple addition of a gold wire mesh or satin ribbon, and perhaps a few sprigs of pine, is all that is needed to create a most appealing present.

ribbon gift pouches

Fill these teeny-tiny pouches with small tokens of affection for thoughtful party favors. Or turn them into charming tree decorations—just use a longer ribbon to tie the bags closed and make a loop with the ends for hanging. For the bright baubles, use tiny tree balls, gold or silver jingle bells, or silky tassels. A sewing machine makes the work go faster, but making them by hand with a needle and thread can be a relaxing pastime. And while ribbons require almost no cutting and so are easy to work with, small scraps of fancy fabrics would do nicely, too.

Cut the ribbons into 10-inch lengths. For each pouch, match a ribbon with one of contrasting color, design, and width. Center the more narrow ribbon on top of the wider. Glue the ribbons together with two dabs of fabric glue about 2 inches from each end. Fold the ribbon in half, wrong sides together, and stitch up the two sides. Trim the ends with the pinking shears. Thread an ornament through a length of thin ribbon and tie the ribbon around the pouch at the point where the ribbons are glued together.

❖   ❖   ❖

MATERIALS

assortment of decorative ribbon of various widths (1 to 4 inches) and matching thread

miniature ornaments or bells

very thin green and red ribbon

TOOLS

fabric glue

pinking shears

christmas "crackers"

Serve up merriment by laying a Christmas cracker at each plate before your holiday dinner. The traditional crackers go POP! when you open them; these won't make noise, but they can spill out loot suitable for revelry: perhaps a funny paper hat to unfold and wear, a noisemaker like a whistle, and a toy ring or necklace. You could also put hard candies, an ornament, a tiny flip-through book, or other jolly trinket inside. Have your guests tear the crackers apart simultaneously at the start of a meal, the stroke of midnight, or any other festive moment.

1. Cut a cardboard tube 4 or 5 inches long. Cut a piece of crepe paper 8 inches longer than the tube and wide enough to go around it about one and a half times. Fill the tube with goodies and wrap the crepe paper around it, gluing the long side in place. Tie ribbon tightly around each end, leaving about 3 inches excess. For a more secure package, you might want to first wrap a short piece of wire around the crepe paper, then tie the ribbon over it. Repeat to make more crackers.

2. Cut a small rectangle of white paper with the decorative scissors. With the hole punch, punch a tree in the center of the rectangle. Glue a tiny piece of green tissue paper to the center of the cracker. Glue the white cutout paper over the tissue, making a green tree.

MATERIALS

cardboard paper-towel tubes

craft-worthy crepe paper, such as Dennecrepe from Crafter's Choice

ribbon

white paper

green tissue paper

TOOLS

decorative-edged scissors

Christmas-tree decorative hole punch

❖ ❖ ❖

gift wrap embellishments

In wrapping, give gifts as much texture as you can. Colored elastic, crepe paper streamers, glass beads, wire, buttons, ribbon, rickrack, and a dose of your creative imagination transform ordinary wrappings into something special. The decorations can be solely for aesthetic delight, or might suggest the gift inside: for instance, twine and sealing wax for a gift of stationery.

▲ To make the straw-mat ribbon: Cut a piece of straw mat slightly more narrow than a wrapped gift and wrap around the package. Finish with a ribbon tied into a bow.

▲ To make the crepe-paper ribbon: Wrap a wide band of crepe paper around a wrapped gift, then wrap wide grosgrain ribbon over the crepe paper and rickrack over the ribbon.

▲ To make the paper-bag wrap: Fold the top of the bag down. Cut a V into the ends of a short length of wide ribbon and drape over the top of the bag. Punch an even number of holes across the top of the bag (including the ribbon) about 1 inch apart. Thread a short length of contrasting ribbon in and out of the holes and tie in knots at both ends.

▲ To make the glass-bead ribbon: Thread beads onto about 20 inches of a long piece of wire. Wrap the unbeaded part of the wire around a wrapped gift, then mold the beaded part into a flower or other shape.

▲ To make the button ribbon: Thread four lengths of thin satin ribbon through the buttons, running each ribbon through two buttons. Position the buttons and ribbon on top of a wrapped gift. Wrap the ribbon ends around the package and glue at the bottom of the package. Glue the buttons in place on the top.

▲ To make the twine ribbon: Wrap twine around a wrapped gift. Use the hot wax and seal to hold the twine in place at the top of the package.

MATERIALS AND TOOLS

decorative gift wrap

ribbon in various styles and widths

FOR THE STRAW-MAT RIBBON: **straw mat (available in specialty paper stores)**

FOR THE CREPE-PAPER RIBBON: **crepe paper, jumbo rickrack**

FOR THE PAPER-BAG WRAP: **colored paper bag; hole punch**

FOR THE GLASS-BEAD RIBBON: **small beads, bead wire; wire cutters**

FOR THE BUTTON RIBBON: **4 large 4-holed buttons; craft glue**

FOR THE TWINE RIBBON: **twine, hot wax and seal**

❖ ❖ ❖

gift wrap designs

Making your own gift wrap from plain paper is a great holiday do-ahead project. Stock up on supplies and invite friends over for an afternoon of creative fun. If a design is complicated, practice before decorating a wrapped gift.

▲ To make the snowflake wrap: Wrap a gift in solid-colored paper. Make snowflakes out of white paper (see page 29) and glue to the wrapped package.

▲ To make the handpainted wraps: Wrap a gift in kraft paper. Lightly trace a stencil design on all sides with a pencil. Paint the design on each side, allowing the paint to dry before painting another side. Or stencil the recipient's monogram on one side of a wrapped gift.

▲ To make the corrugated wrap: Wrap a gift in kraft paper. Cut six pieces of corrugated paper slightly smaller than the sides of the package and glue in place. Tie pieces of twine around the package so there is a tie on each side.

▲ To make the stamped wraps: Wrap a gift in solid-colored paper. Make a stamp by cutting a shape from the craft foam with the X-Acto knife and gluing it to a slightly larger piece of foam. Apply paint to the stamp and press firmly onto the wrapped package. Or stamp candy-cane, teddy bear, or swirly forms on a wrapped gift with rubber stamps and an ink pad. Tie with twine.

▲ To make the sponge-painted bag: Paint the paper bag using a cut-up piece of sponge. Let dry. Paint the clothespin in a contrasting color and let dry. Clip the bag closed with the clothespin.

❖   ❖   ❖

MATERIALS AND TOOLS

colored paper, gift wrap, and kraft paper

twine and ribbon

FOR THE SNOWFLAKE WRAP: white paper; craft glue

FOR THE HANDPAINTED WRAPS: stencil, acrylic paint; brush

FOR THE CORRUGATED WRAP: corrugated paper; craft glue

FOR THE STAMPED WRAPS: craft foam and acrylic paint (or rubber stamps and ink pad); X-Acto knife, craft glue

FOR THE SPONGE-PAINTED BAG: paper bag, acrylic paint, wooden clothespin; sponge

felt gift bags

Instead of using ordinary wrapping paper, make a felt envelope (and save a tree in the process). Both the CD envelope and the lunch bag become part of the present, to be used again and again.

▲ To make the CD envelope: Cut a 6 x 5½-inch piece of red felt and a 6 x 12-inch piece of green felt. With the red thread, sew a 6-inch end of the red felt to a 6-inch end of the green felt, overlapping the pieces by about ½ inch. Fold the green felt back on itself, so the unsewn end covers the stitched end by about ½ inch. With green thread, sew along the two sides, creating a pocket with a red flap on top. With the pinking shears, trim the two sides of the pocket and cut the red flap into a triangle. Fold the flap over and sew the button on the flap near the tip with embroidery thread. Glue the Velcro coin at the same point on the other side of the flap.

▲ To make the lunch-bag-style bag: From the red felt, cut two 5⅜ x 8¼-inch pieces for the front and back, two 3 x 8¼-inch pieces for the sides and one 5⅜ x 3-inch piece for the bottom. Baste the front to the sides, then to the bottom, ¼ inch from the edge. Machine stitch ⅛ inch from the edge. Repeat with the back, basting first, then stitching. Baste the sides to the bottom, then stitch ⅛ inch from the edge. Remove the basting threads, and trim all threads closely. With the hole punch, punch a hole in the center of the bag front, about 1 inch from the top. Add an eyelet. Repeat for the back of the bag.

Cut out a 2½-inch square of white felt with the pinking shears. Punch a hole in one corner and add an eyelet. Cut out a monogram of red felt and glue onto the white square. Thread the ribbon through the felt tag, then thread both ends through the two eyelets of the bag and tie in a bow at the back.

❖   ❖   ❖

MATERIALS

½ yard red felt and matching thread

½ yard green felt and matching thread

white button

green embroidery thread

one Velcro coin (use the hook [fuzzy] side only)

3 eyelets

scrap white felt

25 inches ⅜-inch-wide ribbon

TOOLS

pinking shears

fabric glue

hole punch

gift cards
and tags

Homemade gift cards and tags are the heartfelt finishing touch for any present. Snowmen, country hearts, stars, and evergreens are traditional holiday themes—this is the one time of year when it's fine to be totally sentimental. Copy these examples outright, or use them to inspire your own one-of-a-kind creations.

▲ To make the beaded star card: Thread beads onto a 20-inch length of wire and shape it into a star, leaving a bit of wire at the end for hanging. Fold a rectangle of white cardstock in half to make a card. Cut a piece of red cardstock to fit the inside of the card on the right side and glue in place. Cut two pieces of corrugated paper to fit the front and back of the card and glue in place. With the X-Acto knife and ruler, cut out a square (or other shape) from the front piece, making sure it is larger than the beaded star. Punch a hole in the top of the front piece and hang the star from it. Thread a ribbon through the hole and tie in a bow at the top.

▲ To make the ball ornament card: Fold a large rectangle of green cardstock in half to make a card. Cut a circle of red construction paper. Cut a small rectangle of silver paper and trim one end with the decorative scissors. Glue the circle and rectangle to the front of the card, tucking the rectangle under the circle. Fold a short length of wire in a loop and glue above the silver piece. Use rickrack to decorate the ornament.

▲ To make the snowman tag: Make a snowman out of white and black paper and glue to the luggage tag. Cut a piece of vellum to the same

MATERIALS AND TOOLS

cardstock and construction paper in various colors

ribbon and string

FOR THE BEADED STAR CARD: **glass beads, beading wire, corrugated paper; wire cutters, craft glue, X-Acto knife, metal-edged ruler, hole punch**

FOR THE BALL ORNAMENT CARD: **silver paper, wire, rickrack; decorative-edged scissors, craft glue, wire cutters**

FOR THE SNOWMAN TAG: **green luggage tag (from office supply stores), vellum; craft glue, hole punch**

FOR THE BUTTON TAG: **hole punch**

FOR THE CHECKERBOARD TREE CARD: **semi-opaque patterned paper (from specialty paper stores); craft glue**

FOR THE MONOGRAM IN GLASSINE TAG: **glassine envelope; hole punch**

size as the luggage tag and attach to the tag with a dab of glue at the top. Punch a hole in the vellum where the tag hole is, and thread with a piece of string or ribbon.

▲ To make the button tag: Cut a circle of cardstock and punch four holes in a square in the middle and one hole at the top. Thread string in a cross pattern through the four holes, then, from the back, through the top hole. Tie around the gift's ribbon.

▲ To make the checkerboard tree card: Fold a rectangle of white cardstock in half to make a card. Cut a tree shape of green construction paper and glue to the front of the card. Cut a piece of semi-opaque paper to the same size as the card front and glue on with a few dabs of glue. Decorate the paper with small pieces of red construction paper.

▲ To make the monogram in a glassine envelope: Cut a monogram initial of construction paper just large enough to fit in the envelope. Put the monogram in the envelope and punch a hole in the envelope near the top. Thread ribbon through the hole and tie.

❖ ❖ ❖

more gift cards
and tags

To save time during the busy holiday season, make greeting cards from prefolded cardstock purchased at an art store. For the gift tags, set aside pretty paper and the corrugated packing sheets that cushion boxes of cookies, candy, and crackers, and use decorative-edged scissors to give anything you cut a fancy border.

▲ To make the house card: Make a house-shaped stamp by cutting a form (we used a cookie cutter as a guide) from the craft foam with the X-Acto knife and gluing it to a slightly larger piece of foam. Apply paint to the stamp and stamp the image onto a piece of handmade paper. When dry, tear the paper into a square, using the side of a ruler as a guide. Fold a rectangle of green cardstock in half to make a card. Glue the handmade paper to the front of the card. Cut construction paper into door, wreath, and bow shapes and glue to the handmade paper.

▲ To make the sewn-heart card: Fold a rectangle of brown cardstock in half to make a card and trim the sides with the zigzag scissors. Cut hearts from the fabric scraps and glue to the front of the card with dabs of glue. Open the card up and machine stitch the hearts to the front with thread.

▲ To make the snowflake quilt card: Fold a rectangle of red cardstock in half to make a card. Cut small squares from white construction paper. With the decorative hole punch, punch a snowflake in each square. Use the squares and punched-out snowflakes to glue a checkerboard pattern on the front of the card.

MATERIALS

cardstock and construction paper in various colors

string, twine, and ribbon

FOR THE HOUSE CARD: craft foam and acrylic paint (or stamp and ink pad), handmade paper (or other thin paper); X-Acto knife, craft glue

FOR THE SEWN-HEART CARD: fabric scraps, thread; zigzag-edged scissors, craft glue

FOR THE SNOWFLAKE QUILT CARD: jumbo snowflake decorative hole punch, craft glue

FOR THE CHECKERBOARD TAG: decorative paper, green luggage tag (from office supply stores); craft glue, X-Acto knife, hole punch

FOR THE PRESENT-STYLE TAG: metal-rimmed paper key ring, letter rubber stamps and ink pad, corrugated cardboard; craft glue, hole punch

FOR THE CHRISTMAS-TREE TAG: green oak tag, sticker dots; hole punch

▲ To make the checkerboard tag: Cut a piece of the decorative paper to the same size as the luggage tag. Glue the paper to the tag after cutting a shape out of it with the X-Acto knife. Punch a hole in one end of the tag and thread with string or twine.

▲ To make the present-style tag: Remove the key-holding part from the key ring and discard or save for another use. With the letter stamps and ink pad, stamp a name on the metal-ringed round tag. Wrap ribbon around a square of corrugated cardboard and glue in place. Thread a length of thin string through the hole in the round tag and tie it around the ribbon. Punch a hole in the cardboard and thread with a piece of twine to tie to the gift.

▲ To make the Christmas tree tag: Cut a Christmas tree shape from a piece of oak tag. Decorate the tree with sticker dots or small pieces of paper. Punch a hole at the top of the tree and thread with a piece of white string.

❖   ❖   ❖

index

Acknowledgments

Crafts on pages 29, 43, 45, and 94 created
by Ellen Goldberg;

page 30 by Leslie Hemmings;

pages 33 and 34 by Elizabeth Burdick;

pages 37, 48, 80, and 100 by Robin Tarnoff;

page 44 by Amy Leonard;

pages 46, 69, 70, 97, 98, 103, and 105 by Allison Meyler;

pages 73, 76, and 79 by Morna Crites-Moore;

pages 89 and 93 by Maria Kessel.